Behind the Curtain

Carly Balog

BookLeaf Publishing

India | USA | UK

Presentation by *BookLeaf Publishing*

Web: www.bookleafpub.com

E-mail: info@bookleafpub.com

ISBN: 9789358736410

First edition 2023

ACKNOWLEDGEMENT

I would like to first thank my mom for being my biggest supporter and cheerleader. Without your encouragement, I would not have had the courage to partake in the writing challenge that allowed this book to happen. You have always supported me in my pursuits of being an artist no matter the medium.

Josh, my brother, thank you for always having my back. If mom is my first cheerleader, you are my second and just as important.

Thank you to Ruth for becoming a mentor figure for me. You always find ways to challenge me and push me to become better as both a person and an actor. You are the aspiration of what I want to become as a leader when its my turn.

Thank you to my theater dad figures Sam, Gig, and Twist. Always being there for me as a beacon of support even outside of the theater world as much as you do for your own kids.

Dr. Hoche and Dr. Criniti, Thank you for being the teachers I aspire to be like. You both sparked a passion for me in the world of literature when I would have my doubts. You always have given your supports in my love for Drama and Literature and that it will take me far.

PREFACE

This selection of poems was written for Bookleaf Publishing's #TheWriteAngle Writing Challenge.

This book is a love letter to both of my passions Drama and Literature. I took this as a challenge as a writer to work in a medium format that I was not all that comfortable with. It was creatively fulfilling to challenge myself in this way and to do something I usually wouldn't do.

Audition

It begins.
The show waiting to be filled
with its future performers.

Everybody seemingly running around,
making sure everything is ready.

Directors putting together their stage.
Stage Managers organizing paperwork of
various kinds.
Actors, with resumes and headshots, preparing
either their monologues or grabbing fellow
actors to practice the selected scenes

Each performer having a small amount of time.
They all want to make that impression,
They all want one of the parts.

The excitement in the air is contagious once its
all over.
With all their notes, the director has much to
think on.

Waiting, waiting.... And more waiting

Such a dreadful time.
No matter how many times an actor auditions,
This period is always the worse.

Tick tock, tick tock....

The unknown.
What decisions are being made?
How much longer will this have to be endured?

Tick tock, tick tock....

Was that an email notification? Check it again
for whatever amount of time.
Oh well, keep watching the clock tick by.

All that can be done is to wait...

And wait...

Cast List

This day is such a mix of emotions.
Nervousness, Excitement, Dread, and many
more to come.

Some frantically checking emails,
Some checking for a physical copy.
Just wait for some kind of news

Finally an announcement!
The Cast List is out!

Everybody rushes to find out.
Some are excited,
They have been cast.
They got the part they wanted.
Some are disappointed.
They didn't get what they were hoping for.
Others are devastated,
These are the ones not cast at all.

So much going on with everyone at one time.
Its almost a mad house with all of the reactions.

At least the show can officially start.

Design

This is where the non-actors, the designers, get
to have some fun.
Set, Costume, Lights, Props.
All of them come together for the first point in
the show process.
They put their heads together to think.
The creativity in the room is amazing.

They confer with the director.
It is necessary so their vision can come across.
SMs scribbling everything down to keep track of
everything.

The point it happens is never linear.
Sometimes it starts before auditions,
Sometimes after.

Their inspirations come from everywhere.
A concept could be anything:
A word,
An emotion.
Something physical,
Something psychological.
Endless ideas from all involved.

If one thought the actor's creativity was
contagious and inspiring,
The designers light a passion under everyone's
butts.

First Readthrough

The first of many rehearsals to come.
The excitement in the air is contagious.

Scripts being passed out,
Everyone sitting around in a circle.
Pencils and Highlighters in hand.

Actors reading the script from beginning to end.
For some its the first they've read it,
For others who knows how many times.
Highlighters scribbling as they go,
making sure they get all of their lines.
Giggles and laughter,
maybe some tears depending on the story.

When the night is over, and everyone has else
gone home...
The Director thinks to themselves,
"This is going to be a great show."

First Blocking

The first time since getting the script to move
around the acting area.
Going from beginning to end,
actors stumble along.

They follow where they're told to go.
Both SM's and Actors frantically writing in the
margins.

Its less about the acting and more placement.
Remember to mark everything in pencil.
The things told in this rehearsal mostly never
stay that way.

There's excitement in the air.
But the director can't wait for this beginning part
to pass quickly.

Early Rehearsals

This is where the early work happens.
Scripts still in hand,
Stumbling through the scenes.
Some are easier to get through than others.

Blocking not set stone.
Hurried eraser sounds followed by hurried
scribbles to change it.

Actors still developing the characters.
What motivates them?
What mannerisms they have?
How they talk?
How they move through the space?

For the director, off book couldn't come soon
enough.
Quick conversations with both SM and
designers for future notes.
For the SM, they're just praying they get all the
changes and information down.

This time passes quicker than one would think.

The Set

One of the more well known design areas.

The setting.
The background.
Where everything takes place.

It frames the actors,
The play seems more real with it.

Like costumes, they're fluid fitting the needs of
the show.
It could be a house or apartment.
An old castle or place in the future.
Even just benches and tables that let the
imagination run wild.

The possibilities for the setting is endless.

The Costumes

Probably the most recognizable of design.

Bringing the characters to life with their
clothing.
They give much insight to personalities.

They also place the actors with in the right
period.
From Greek to Medieval,
To Shakespeare to Present day.
Even in times far beyond ourselves.
One costume off could mess everything up.

The amount of work is un-measurable
Needs of costumes pending on needs of the
show.
Custom pieces might be needed,
Historically accurate,
Or even just quantity.

We all know how the clothes make the man (or
woman or them).

The Props

Its not like the set.
Putting you into the environment,
Where the show is placed.

Its not like the costumes.
The physical clothes.
The personalities of each character.

It is its own category.
They are the physical things around the set.
Items specifically chosen to be played with,
Interacted with the actors.
A toy in a sense that has a purpose.
Their usage essential to whatever goes on in the
show.

The great part is they could be anything:
A phone,
A sword,
A magic book,
A ball,
And so much more.

The Lights

While the set and costumes put their actors in
their environment,
the thing that sets the mood is the lights.

It illuminates the stage, both literally and
figuratively.
It changes the shows world based on the
arrangement.

Floods illuminate everything and making sure
all are seen on the stage.
Spotlights pull the attention to a specific person,
group, or area.
Gels or Colored LEDs create a mood with the
color it emits.
And thats just the beginning.

It pulls everything together
It makes the show feel almost performance
ready for those involved.

Stage lights is like the sun for a performer.
Warm, inviting, and the light of their path.

Off Book

Such a dreaded time.
Probably the most unsteadied rehearsal, even for
the most experienced.

The loss of the script in hand is heavy.
Its almost a comfort at this point.

Its the first time to rehearse with no script.
Words unsure, calling for line.
Where do hands go?
Where to move to?

Actors doubting themselves on knowledge.
Its rough, both to watch and to perform.
They make it through, but its full of hiccups.

Middle Rehearsals

The show is starting to come together.

Its where everything falls to place,
All the pieces coming together.

Scripts out of hand, actors do their magic.
The setting coming to alive piece by piece.
Costumes starting to dress everyone.
Things to fiddle and to explore.
All the little nuances coming go life.
Probably the closest to what the show will look
before the final touches made.
Its where most of the magic comes.

How exciting to see it all come together.

Tech Week

Every actors least favorite time.

The week of the show opening.
All of the last final details coming together.

Stage Managers calling the show with the cues
in order.
Directors watching from afar to make sure
everything comes together
Actors, dressed in full costumes, performing the
show start to finish.
Stage hands running around for the first time
behind the scenes.
There's alot to come together all in a week.
Sometimes the director can't help but stop but
they know they shouldn't.

Its a frustrating experience for everyone
involved.

Its called "Hell Week" for a reason after all.

Cue to Cue

The most frustrating part of the whole
experience.

This night isn't for the actors.
Its for the tech running the show.

Stage Managers calling the show for the first
time, starting from Cue 1 to the end.
Board Operators learning for the first time what
buttons they need to press.
Stage Hands learning where stuff gets placed
and rearranged.

Its a lot of stopping and starting.
Adjusting things as they go, wanting everything
to be perfect.

Cue X, go...
Place item down,
Change the lights,
Play that Sound
Reset for Cue x

Over and Over til every cue is done.

Final Dress

So much nervousness running through everyone.
The show opens tomorrow.
This is the last rehearsal.

So many little things to worry about.
Will I get this moment right?
Will I get this out on stage correctly?
Will this quick change work?
And so many more will I/won't I floating in the
air.

Sometimes the director wishes they had more
time.
Just one more rehearsal.
One more week even.

At the end, the director addresses their actors.
The show is now theirs and out of the director's
hands.
Its going to be a great show.

You know what they say,
A bad final dress makes a great opening.

Opening Night

The night that everyone has waited for.
Everything that came before, lead to this day.

In the front of house, the audience comes.
They pile in, awaiting for their entertainment
patiently.
Some of them are family members,
Some may be friends.
Others that may just love the art,
And others thats never seen one before.

Behind the stage, the actors also wait.
Either in the dressing room, or in the wings.
They wait for the call to get in their places.
All of them a mix of emotions...
Nervous, but excited for what's to come.

Before they know it, the time has come.
All of their hard work ready to be shown.
The lights come up and they're on stage.

The atmosphere is almost electric.
Both groups feeding off each other.
More reactions from the audience,
Leads to the actors to giving it their all.

At the end comes the most gratifying sound for
any performer.
The cheers and the applause.
The actors bow in gratitude.

It finally happened.
The Show is Open.

Closing Night

The emotions are similar to that of opening and
the other performances.
This time though,
There's a bitterness that reigns heavy.

Its the last night, and after tonight it will be over.

So many last things.
The last curtain rise and last lights up
The last for that funny moment
The last of that costume quick change.
Just so many lasts.

As they get closer to the end, everyone's a little
anxious.
Its no suprise with the time put in.
They knew this time was coming since the
beginning, all involved did.

When the final bow comes, its bittersweet.
The cheers, while rewarding as they are, it
reminds them the show is closing.
All their hard work now coming to a close.

There is no tomorrow with the production.
The Show has closed.

Tear Down

If Closing Night is bittersweet,
this moment is even more heartbreaking.

Its time to take everything down.
Many hands make light work.

Break down the set piece by piece.
The sound of power tools ring in the air.
As more screws come out, more pieces come
apart.

The Costumes and Props get separated.
Each piece of the two groups moved by
whomever to where it needs to.

Once the stage is bare and empty,
It all sinks in.
Its over.
While the show technically already ended,
Its official now.

Its the end of the show.

Post Show

After everything is over,
this moment can't be prepared for.

Its not like the bustle of auditions,
All the excitement for what's to come.
Its not like the stress of tech week,
The worry that the work will not be good.
Even with closing night and all its sadness,
This moment is not one to anticipate.

Its not even an emotion at all.
Its more of a void, an emptiness.
Just nothing.

The show has passed,
There's nothing to do.
No place to go.
No audience to perform for.
Nothing to prepare for.

Sure later actors will evaluate everything...
What they did wrong, What was right?
Could they have done more?
Will they keep going in this world?
Will they stop all together?

So many should ofs and could ofs...
But for now at this moment,
Just nothing...

The Cycle Continues

After so long, it all starts over again.

A new show is gonna start.
Directors and Stage Managers gathering all
everything need.
Designers putting their ideas to paper.
Actors preparing their materials to impress.

As one show ends,
Another starts.
It never ends.

Isn't it wonderful how it continues?
Always on the way to the next work.
Always circling through stages, Always cycling.

www.ingramcontent.com/pod-product-compliance
Lightning Source LLC
LaVergne TN
LVHW010849200726

843508LV00012B/2820